I hope it's not over, and good-by.

Everette Maddox

Selected Poems

Edited with an Introduction by

Ralph Adamo

ISBN:1-60801-000-7
ISBN 13: 978-1-60801-000-4
Library of Congress Control Number: 2009930395

Book design by Kelcy D. Wilburn
Cover design by Alex Dimeff
Cover image: ca. 1978, by Lindsay Bach, © 2009 by Lindsay Bach; used by permission.

Scanned images of bar napkin and coaster drafts on frontis page and on 156 courtesy of the Historic New Orleans Collection; used by permission.

Scan of the *Atlantic* rejection letter and pages from the c. 1972 story "The Animal Fair" at the end of the book are courtesy Celia Maddox; used by permission.

University of New Orleans Publishing
Managing Editor, Bill Lavender
http://unopress.org

Dead more than twenty years now, Everette Maddox remains very present to those who knew him, and, through his poems, will surely become a presence to many more who never had that pleasure. The editor and publishers of this volume wish to thank especially the publishers of his four books of poems for their collegiality in making work available for this reproduction and for the vision they demonstrated by publishing his work in the first place. Everette would be generous in his own thanks to that faithful group and to the many editors of journals and small magazines who chose to share the delight they experienced upon encountering his poems. For a full accounting of where each poem was published, in periodicals or books, please see the Acknowledgments & Permissions at the end of the book.

Contents

Editor's Introduction

The Publishing History

Everette Maddox's first collection was a chapbook issued by the Xavier University Press in New Orleans, called *The Thirteen Original Poems*. He had moved to the city from a long tenure as a graduate student at the University of Alabama to take a one-year appointment as poet-in-residence at Xavier; the year was 1976, thus the title.

In 1982, Maxine Cassin's New Orleans Poetry Journal Press published *The Everette Maddox Songbook*, a selection of work from four book-length manuscripts. Maddox and Cassin made their table of contents after a process that included consultation with a number of his poet friends.

In 1988, and in failing health, Everette worked with Hank Staples and Bill Roberts to put out his third book, *Bar Scotch*, under their new Pirogue Publishing label. *Bar Scotch* rounded up many of the poems not used in the *Songbook*, including portions of a sonnet sequence to the woman, Holly, who had captured his imagination at the time of the *Songbook*, and to whom that collection is dedicated. *Bar Scotch* is dedicated to his brother Bill, also a writer, who had recently given up tenure to move to New Orleans, drink, and write.

During Maddox's last twelve months (he died in February of 1989), he had begun writing regularly again for the first time in some years, poems with a distinctively more vernacular sound to them, and fewer obvious formal elements. Portals Press, run by John Patrick Travis, organized a group of Maddox's friends to sort through those final poems, generally still in handwritten form, and edit them into a posthumous collection, *American Waste*, published in 1993.

In 2004, another group of friends (led by Bob Woolf and Celia Lewis), based in Maddox's home turf of Alabama, gathered to assemble a book made up of poems not included in other books, the majority of them from three named manuscripts but including a sizable 'uncollected' section of poems, some of which appear to date from the lost '80s. "Shades Mountain," Maddox's early '70s *New Yorker*-published poem, makes its first book appearance in that volume, *Rette's Last Stand*, which begins with an introduction by his old friend and one-time protégé, Rodney Jones.

In addition to the poetry collections, Maddox has had a lively on-line presence since his death, especially on a site maintained by Bob Wolfe and Wolfe's son. His life and work are also the focus of a 1994 issue of *New Orleans Review* edited by me, and a 2006 book, *Umpteen Ways of Looking at a Possum* (Xavier University Press), edited by Julie Kane and Grace Bauer.

The Body of Work

Everette Maddox's poetry and the legends that have grown up around him suggest the need for a serious biography. While he lived a more public life than most poets (forced into public places as much by years of homelessness as by choice), the 'real' Everette Maddox remains concealed in the myth, obscured by pipe smoke and alcohol fumes, by the inevitable projections upon him by those who knew him and those who have only heard the stories. We each have our own Everette, and then we have the poems.

In order to begin talking about them, we do need to refer once again to his life. It was a life that illustrates (while demonstrating) contradictory visions of the artist. On one hand, he was entranced by and wished to emulate an idea of glamour (as portrayed by Scott and Zelda, for one example that contains the seeds of its own contradiction). On the other hand, he was chronically broke, out of work (and not much interested in getting into it), homeless (not only literally), under the influence (from drink served in places that would not be mistaken for glamorous) and— in his case, in the end— literally starving. And/but Maddox was, too, the 'professional,' the conservative (in taste and with no obvious interest in politics), the one to whom clothes and manners mattered, whether or not he could maintain appearances in either regard. His poetry also bears the distinction of being almost entirely about himself and the life he was living, spoken in a voice that was unmistakably the poet pretending to be no one other than himself.

It is true that in each of the things his friends have written about him one may find the truth, as well as an affection that is as real and painful as it can be. But do we find Everette there? Not really. He is, rather, cagily ensconced in his own words to a degree that is remarkable.

Maddox's poetry moved and changed, of course— moved over time from a somewhat detached and humorous posture to a profoundly entangled and humorous posture, while his concerns remained pretty constant. As Jones writes in *Rette's Last Stand*, "After love and directly linked to it, decadence in all its forms, appealed to him, so he did not just suffer his decline, he relished it." In one memorable conversation in the early '80s, during which Everette could not cease expressing his misery in elegant and heart-breaking language, and during which he reasserted his occasional threat of suicide, I suggested that if he was going to go that way he ought to at least hop a train to the West Coast, enjoy three days of drinking against the American landscape and then jump in the ocean when he was done. "That would send the wrong message," he replied sadly. (In the end, he died of esophageal cancer, in his case, particularly, a lifestyle-related disease. Needless to say, he had no health insurance, nor any clear access to medical care; his death came only a few days following his admittance to the city's Charity Hospital, since closed by Katrina.)

More to the point, I suppose, is the observation that even as Maddox materially changed from a thin but contained and dapper man into an emaciated and somewhat wilder form, so did his poetry change, bodily: from what most would recognize as related to the prosodic traditions of English-language poetry to a poetry that embraced the vernacular with all its unpredictability and plain-spokenness. While Maddox never enunciated a poetics that included the idea of relaxing the hold of traditional form on his work, that is what happened, even as his voice, the essential Maddox, remained largely unchanged. It is a journey made in the poetry of many mid-century Americans— Merwin, Lowell, James Wright (especially the latter)— less an embrace of free-verse than a sort of arrival at his own version of the language. In Maddox's case in the late poems taken from *American Waste*, we can see, especially, a poet's work exploding within the memory trace of an older idea of form.

This Selection

In choosing this sort of book and these poems to represent Everette Maddox, offering what we hope will be both a reintroduction to his public and an opportunity for those who missed him to find and enjoy the best work of a fine American poet, the publishers and I have decided to produce a selected volume. It is intended as a showcase of his styles, concerns, his wit and sometimes dazzling sensibility, to display some of the many profound moments of poetry he produced in what was finally a short and frequently unhappy life. My criteria for selecting among the poems would be difficult to articulate. My re-readings produced new gut reactions to every poem, and I was guided by those reactions as well as my memory of earlier reactions, and sometimes of hearing his voice declaiming the poem. (He was a great reader of his own work, capable of making magic in the spark between voice and word.) Finally, there are a couple of *categories* of poem that I trimmed out of this selection, leaving, I think, sufficient representatives. Those would be poems which conclude with a lovelorn Maddox producing a sort of embittered, ironic last line, as well as the poems of gleeful confusion, usually over some flaw in the language or our way of mishandling same.

It is my hope and assumption that we will have a collected poems within a reasonable time, and that it will include not only the work in the four books from which this selection was made, but also work, newly found, that as yet remains lost in various places. It was not easy leaving a coherent legacy when he had no place to call home and no place to collect and organize his body of work. I anticipate as well collections of letters and the biography that some exceptional chronicler will one day undertake.

For now, let me note that I have only loosely tried to organize this selection by chronology or even by book. Since the poems were not written generally in an order suggested by the first two or last of the current four volumes, I felt free to improvise other associations for these poems besides just time of composition or date of publication, though the last many poems come exclusively from *American Waste*. I hope the way they are presented enhances the experience of reading them. But even if it does not in any way do that, the poems speak with eloquence, frequently brilliantly, on their own and need no dressing up. For anyone interested in seeing which poems were originally published in which collection, an appendix is provided.

A final thought, supported by these poems, but belonging perhaps more to a future biography than to this collection: In extraordinary ways, Everette Maddox was a free man. He simply did not have the concerns and attachments of ordinary people, though he was in his own odd way a complete populist. It was this detachment— despite gripes, complaints, and genuine sorrow— that drew people to him, I believe. Especially creative people, most of whom remained torn between their commitment to their art and the desire to succeed, or at least survive. Not Everette. It's hard to believe he ever gave a serious thought to survival. The truest expression of this wondrous indifference can be found in the later poems, from *American Waste*, most of which were composed in his last year at the bar of the Maple Leaf.

I am looking at the moment at a photograph of my old friend, my companion through many afternoons and evenings of drink and talk, of survival in the margins. He looks surprised. Perplexed. Amused. About to speak.

Ralph Adamo
New Orleans
December 17, 2008 – July 27, 2009

I hope it's not over,
and good-by.

Stealing a Boat: April, 1968

Good things tend to explode
In their gratuity— so the boat exploded,
And the whole idea of stealing it.
That Sunday afternoon we found it, stuck in a cove,
Back in stagnant water, chained to a dogwood tree.

Two nights later we were back,
Ready with a hacksaw (stolen, too, to make it complete)
And a borrowed lantern; but the boat was gone.
We swore, hunted the swamps, stopping to eye
Fish squirming obscurely, and a few fireflies.

Not far up the river we found it again.
Below a steep bank, chained again. It had to be good
Enough to keep being chained. It took us
A slow twenty minutes hacking to get it loose.
We tossed the chain in, and shoved out dizzily.

It was strange to be in the middle of water, muddy
As the water was, cloudy as the night was— the moon
An innuendo behind the clouds— stranger to me,
Who didn't know how to swim. The oars were whittled
Two-by-fours: we kept turning around at first.

We learned how to row, though, by taking different sides
And the same side to keep it straight… Logs stuck
Out like snouted serpents. From the dark shore
The noise of critters blurred. We got off on a barge
And swiped two life preservers— cows scared us back.

The Northport Bridge was a row of lights ahead
In the slow water that had started to catch spring rain;
We headed for it. Watery enterprise ours, we rowed

Tired past caring, the shore swimming by faster now—
Not even a laconic hoot-owl disparaged us.

Mere April our impulse, still, though not pursued,
Probably, by either constable or haint,
We had the rowing to do, the huge spring night
To row against... In that disordered flight
We shared Huck's terrible integrity.

Black Humor

To Nickey Lewis

Alas, poor Yorick: his head's in the wrong place.
Only this callow man can dig him now
who leans on his spade and sings.
Object, not subject, Yorick's head
Grins dust.
Subject goes underground, and what's unearthed
by comic chance is this:
the brilliant shape we juggle in the hand,
not heavy at all.
The back he bore me on lies out of sight,
divorced from mirth
that was not infinite, after all.
Nothing's together, because
When consciousness is out, everything's out,
Unless somebody yawns profundities.
Look here, Horatio:
he needed eyes to glimmer from these sockets
that now show black as loam.
Chap, fallen,
He's given back neck and thigh and hip to earth,
and now
somebody has to hold his head up for him.
Back was not where it was,
though once I tittered there.
The holes we stop are finally where we are.
Granted soliloquies
are silly, shattering as they do against
cold palace walls:
so is our last grave home, Horatio
silly and cold, I mean
and the best gives echo only out of skulls.
Lithe worms bore in Yorick's grinning head.
The only things that can happen to heads are obscene.

To the Girl I Love from an Office Window

I can see you from my office window
Every Wednesday morning when
You cross the street to check your mail
And come out, started home again.

All winter, when the tall trees were
Just leafless poles, I watched you walk
To the corner; hollered once, and waved:
A window's not much place to talk.

Late in March it snowed, and you
Struggled by in that pink coat you wear,
Your face red in the cold. A few
Flakes whirled up and hit your hair.

I asked you out in April; of course
You were tied up. Now, first of May,
The trees are too heavy with green to let
Me watch you long, to let you stay

In sight. Today you yank from a shrub
A handful of leaves— some seasonal scheme.
I watch you first, then just your legs,
Till the tall trees hide you deep as a dream.

Shades Mountain

Here where a mass of autumn trees
rises to the left like a wall of red
and to the right iron ore
shudders away, what if I swerve to the right
suddenly, hauling the little car
and my friend and me over the desperate edge
beyond the expected motive,
lumbering through the green and bitter red
of Pyracantha, careening down to burst
like destiny on Birmingham,
pocking the tranquil campus with the smoke
and flare of my decision?
What would it matter to either of us?
If I am my friend's keeper, what could I do
kinder for him than to drag his life,
stubborn and sad like mine, along with mine
fluttering like a pennant into the dark?

Nature is not for us— things open up
on every hand, open onto the cliffs
sheer as the one blind Gloucester thought he fell from.

I have sat alone in a room at night
with one lamp, hearing outside
huge trees shake in the belligerent wind,
and thought that if I walked out on the porch
for a moment only, to watch leaves flail
the corner light, the wind
would tear me instantly apart.
The wind would tear us all apart
and scatter us like leaves, like dead leaves
through the uncaring streets.
Nature is not for us— but I do not plunge

us into that dream of nature....
I groan in second over the top,
around the curve, and plunge
down to the left in the secret pines
where rich men's houses glow
and their daughters pace in the coming dark.

Green Girl, Green Ice Cream

To the Memory of Wallace Stevens

The girl behind the drugstore counter may
Or may not know her ice cream is as green,
And the same shade of green, as her dress. To play
Colors off thus is human business: seen
At the drug store now, at the Chukker later, where
The catsup bottle is as red, and the same
Red as the girl's loud shirt, and Hog Doo's hair
Is as yellow as his beer. We have no name
For such occurrences. You never asked
Their names. But you could have twirled
These colors like batons: for so you basked
In the accidental harmony of the world.

"No New Tabs"

Sign in the Chukker, October 25th, 1971

When the stranger swung into this dark
butt-littered bar, draped his white
weird toga, or whatever, over a stool,
and ordered Miller's Malt, no one was
perturbed (it being late, and most of us dead
drunk). But when he said "No bread,"
a hush fell like a flatiron. "No new tabs,"
Mark said, and gestured. The stranger
scratched his beard, his blue eyes slow
and casual as swimming pools.
"Lookee here," said the stranger, "I don't know
how long it takes you necks to get the papers,
but I'm the son of God, and I could turn
this Miller into wine; but I'm inclined
to turn you and your buddies into Ovaltine.
What do you say? I'm kind of in a hurry."
One skinny arm reached out of Mark's white shirt,
shaking, and tore the sign down.
A row of white teeth chattered and chattered, and said,
"Here at the Chukker,
if nothing else, we believe. More to the point,
you gotta make exceptions. What about another?"
Brushing the sticky halo from his hair,
he went to fetch it.

Balloon Piece

for Michael Benedikt

Behind every great balloon
stands a kid. You know
the type: rumpled and grimy,

belching mud-pies and farting
Kool-Aid; lighting the laundry
bill up like a marquee. Oh

and aren't they pleased
with these shiny sausages
of air! Just pop one: you'd think

a close friend had shown
himself, at last, as nothing
but an empty sailor suit. Or watch

when one gets loose:
eyeballs roll back
like film in a Kodak, fists

clench, breath comes
short, as the old unreal
rises and disappears— where?

Is the sky really up there?

Moon Fragment

A man squats by the railroad tracks tonight
eating a moon fragment: not cheese
at all, but a honeydew melon. His hands
are fuzzy. A train roars past. In the
lighted windows men and women stand
with pewter cups raised. Tea slops out.
Then it is dark again. Moon-eaters have
no time for such foolishness. The silence
is not absolute, though, because the world's
longest accordion, the world's longest
musical expansion bridge, is playing
somewhere. I am up in my office
watching the glitter of my last cigar sail
out the window, over the shrubbery, down
into the darkness where summer is
ending. I keep office hours at night so
nobody comes around to bother me. Not even
you. The moon comes around, though. I want to
drag it down and hand it to you and say, "Here,
this is lovely and useless and it cost me
a lot of trouble. You can tie it up on
the river behind your house, and go down to
look at it whenever you like." The trouble is,
you don't want it tied up, and you are
right. This is no new problem. Eight hundred
years ago a man heads home from the
Fair, pushing a wheelbarrow full of real
moon pies. For ten years he has been
stealing wheelbarrows, and nobody even
suspects. Well, what is all this? you
want to know. Right again. I could
say I don't know myself because the evidence
is not all in, never will be. I could say it's

the unfinished moon poem I've always wanted
to almost write. Well, what is it all about? you
ask. What does it mean? You have me
there. It means, whatever this is between
you and me, I hope it's not over, and good-by.

Lines on His Thirtieth Birthday

On a hill high above
the mild October day
I stand, heroic, hands
clasped behind my back,
as the last musket's
crack fades
and the smoke drifts away
from the place where the famous
Battle of my Youth was fought.

Who won? Who lost?
Who knows? My speech,
which I seem to have misplaced,
tells. Oh well:
myself and loves and grey
uniform were not among
the casualties, quite; though
a gold button dangles.

Now we'll bind the wounds,
free the slaves, and set up
(oh shrewdly!) a shrine
in the decaying mansion
of my body: post cards,
stuffed possums, and, out back,
whiskey to be sold
such emissaries
from the glacial future
as have coin to spend.

Publication

It's not what you
expected. Little
black ants of print
climb up onto
the stiff page
of the literary mag
and form a man.

Horrible! Ants
arranged in the shape
of a bent old man
with a bottle of Tequila
between his knees.

"It's all wrong! He
should have a lard can
on his foot," you say,
banging your foot,
which is stuck in a lard can
made of ants.

Nothing on the page is true,
only the failure.
But that's something, so
you decide it's probably O.K.
some fragment of this funny Bible
has got transcribed
at last.

The Miracle

"Things are tight," the man
said, tightening his
quasi-friendly grin.
"We can't give you a
job, we can't give you
any money, and
we don't want these here
poems either." He
tightened his tie. "Fact
is, the old cosmic
gravy train's ground to
a halt. It's the end
of the line. From now
on, there's going to
be no more nothing."
He went on, lighting
a cigar: "We don't
wish we could help, but
even if we did,
we couldn't. It's not
our fault, by God, it's
just tight all over."
He brought his fist down
on the burnished desk
and lo! from that tight
place there jetted forth
rivers of living water.

The Substance of a Late-Night Phone Call

I have stagnated
for 13 years
in Tuscaloosa,
Alabama, and want
badly to get out.
However, my friend
Bob Woolf in Mobile
tells me he has
left a trail
of stagnation
all over the Southeast,
like a slug. If
not on the road,
where is activity
to be sought?
I know: in the moment.
But how does one
make the moment move?
I imagine us all
standing over our lives
with sticks,
prodding them like
loaded frogs,
hissing "Flies, Dan'l, flies."

Heard (Glider) Poem

Midday Saturday in Spring.
A kid's day, not mine.
I need a screwdriver.
I slump on the creaking glider
of the neighbor's swing set
in the red brick alley
where we live. Blond Joe T.,
my daughter's friend,
stuck to his bike
like a piece of lemon candy,
tells me all second grade
boys are punks.
Remembering, I concur.
Joe T.'s in the first grade.
"My great-grandmother's 92,"
he says, and adds
"She's dead. She lived
to be 92."
I nod grimly, thinking:
That's nothing, Joe T.,
I'm thirty years old
and it looks as if I'll be
on this damn glider forever.

Poem

After everything quits,
things continue
happening. The phone
rings. A knock comes
at the door. Lightning
flashes across the bed
where you bend, looking
at the dictionary.
Asleep, you keep waking
from dreams. The surface
of your life keeps
being broken, less and less
frequently, at random.
Raindrops after a storm:
surprise: the ghost of awe.

The Comfort of Artifice

Eddying in and out of this blue fall day,
I hum like a Hohner. Not that those who
come too close can quite say, in that
cringing moment, whether it's an aria or
some bonafide anguish. Let's just say it's
how I push the morning aside, scared as I
am of silence and trees and the sky— that
parking lot for clouds. It's my answer to
Nature. It's an existential "Steamboat
a-comin'!" It's the comfort of artifice:
a handrail I construct as I go, something
of my own to hang on to, riding the esca-
lator up this unknown afternoon.

Maintenance

It's a thankless task
sweeping up the halls of consciousness.
My friends are all such fools
I can't help liking them.
They want to create or destroy,
and somebody has to just keep order.
These closed doors
emit the sounds of snip-snip-snipping:
my friends are snipping up insights.
They throw the rejects out
through little slots in the doors.
I come along and sweep them up
like ticker-tape, into a gleaming pile.
It's five o'clock now,
and I wouldn't mind hoisting a few
down at Arthur's Bar & Grill;
some of my friends have already gone.
They don't think I have any fun:
they don't know I carry a hip flask
and talk, far into the night, to the rats.

Hypothetical Self-Epitaph

What if I just caved in,
gave out, pulled over
to the side of
the road of life,
& expired like an old
driver's license?
You might say He didn't
get far in 31 years.
But I'd say That's
all right, it was
the world's longest trip
on an empty tank.

Rutledge Youngblood Refuses to Lie Under the Banyan Tree Any More

Rutledge has made up his mind
this is the last day he will lie
at length in his glinting hair
his eye fixed on a fig
his toes alive in the permissive mud.

Out beyond these roots in a pool
clear by day dark by night
purple eels jiggle:
that is another universe of course
but that is not where Rutledge lives
and neither is this.

Though the air is thick with bells
bizarre with flutes
Rutledge lies on his belly now
billowing like a child's balloon
and it means nothing to him
that ultimates and ultimates buoy him up.

He will leave in the morning
by the ordinary door
and walk in the shrill grey streets
in the old soot and sunshine.
He has learned all he needed to know,
what he already knew, that he is happy.

Welcome Home

I understand:
for years, perhaps, you have lived
underground. Handling only
darkness, you have not become
accustomed to it. You want to get out.
One day you find an object which
may be a chair; at any rate,
a surface. Standing on
this dark thing, you reach up.
Here at the top the smell
is oppressive, sweet. You almost
fall. But you push, and the top begins
to crack. Plaster, or something, falls
around you. Emerging, you know
the smell: cake. Noise, lights:
you are outside, standing giddily on the top,
swathed in ribbons. And there
are all your friends,
dressed up, half drunk. The applause
is enormous. It is a party
for you. One of the crowd, the drunkest
and happiest, shrilling through a megaphone
"Welcome home,"
is me.

Poem for Fred: On the Occasion of His Still Being Alive

Think of 247 sequinned porcupines
dragging a windmill down the main street
   of Des Moines.
Why not? You've never been there,
and you can believe it. Think of darkness
crackling like a pregnant pine cone
ruthlessly in the Waffle House parking lot
here in Tuscaloosa.
It is all in excess, and you would never
go to the trouble. It just happens. Think
of yourself, as I do, frog-eyed on the commode
cutting through Fonda posters
like a laser beam, ripping
the flag apart, jerking off over the Muse.
How else can you explain it?
I rode with you, and I was scared,
whirled along, hunched in the eye
of that hurricane of worthlessness.
The speed there was too much.
Harlequin, huckster, free-lance
pisser on the fires of others' passions,
you yelled "Hey bitch you want to ball?"
at every light. The last time
it was my mother. I do not doubt
the first time it was yours. Nor
that you dropped a small tear
into your shirt pocket like a marijuana seed
to be planted later, somewhere.

I was scared, though,
you would jump clear out, pull the ripcord,

and bob cautiously down
into an ocean of filth. I didn't
want to drive my own life. You were as easy
to understand as it was to believe
people were really dead in the cemetery
we cake-walked past in your space machine,
grey as an old man's fingernail
and faster. The gates were locked.
The dead could not get in. Only you, Fred:
you were heavy enough to crash.
You have come home that way
many times, always alone, to the smoldering heap
beneath which your handless heart
ticks like an old, suave porcelain clock.

The Reason Why

My eyes? You don't have
to tell me. I stay
drunk all the time now.
It's on purpose. I'm
drinking myself to
death. Melodrama!
That's why. Because just
living is a dis-
traction. Getting out
of the car, the bed,
the rain, is next to
impossible. And
being drunk makes it
harder, which makes me
mad, which is how I
like it. Because it
never occured to
me that the end of
the world would be so
dull.

The Blast

This December morning,
laboring across
the frozen quad
toward coffee,
head bowed in thought
like a truck
bogged down in a field,
suddenly without
thinking I let rip
a clarion sneeze;
students look up
from car-keys,
dogs from puddles:
the world unfurls
at this bright blast—
a Vivaldi trumpet note.

Monet

The window of my half-
ass job frames a group
of students dripping
across a small yard's
green gloom. No more
rain! because a noose
of sunlight snares them—
skirts & hats
& army jackets— & pulls
them tight, like
a yellow slicker,
retarding their academic
progress. Fixing them
(such a lovely mess!),
making an old man's
day immortal. Water-lilies.

What I Meant

Mary Louise, the waitress
at what my girl-friend's
sister dubbed the Gulp
'n' Vomit, slips me
a couple of Tylenol over
the counter in response to
my groan, overture to
a Friday noon breakfast.
"I brought it on
myself," I say, and she
winks: "I saw you
in here the other night
when you was feeling
no pain— or you *was*."

Yes and No, Mary Louise:
That must have been
the night the booze
miscarried, and I got
numbed outside but
personally locked in
with the Loveless Terrors;
that's what I meant
by snarling over my sweet
roll: "Reach me my whip
and chair in here, and
don't forget the pistol."

Drinking Glass

for Charles Simic

Pick it up and hold it
to the light—
a repository of dust,
hair and lipstick.

An old cigar butt's
capsized in the bottom.

Nonetheless, the glass
retains its shape,
like a stately matron.

Dump it out
(salvaging the butt),
rinse it, twirl it
once on a cloth,
and look! how Clarity
Rides Again.

Raise it now in a toast
to Friendship,
and observe,
deep in the amber booze,
the old bright planets
winking.

Of Rust

It struck me today,
while trying to explain to
a student how he should
go to hell, that all
my languages are rusty.

My French for Graduates,
my old Latin minor, my
Berlitz German— oh
my Esperanto's hopeless.

All my Englishes too,
Old, Middle, Modern,
Pidgin, Basic. In Paris
I asked for a room
dans douche. I can't get

cliches straight: Does
water flow under the dam
or over the bridge?

How will I ever manage to ask you to come
back to me in a sentence with so many
            to's in it?

My fans must be confused
(me too) because "If gold rust,
what will iron do?" (Chaucer)

Somebody said the best
words, in any order,
were *Alone in bed.* E.g.
In bed alone. In alone

bed. Bed alone in. But

I think the best words
are *In bed with you*, and
the best order is
In you with bed. Rust

has its uses: They make
old beds out of it,
like ours you painted
white. I remember too
one winter dawn (this was
before we met), some
friends and I, loaded, drove
the wrong way up a hill

in the fog, and stopped
to hear a small mystery:
birds, creaking like hinges,
saying, it seemed to me,
just what they meant.

Of Fashion

If you don't believe life
is rhythmic, listen
late at night: all over
the world neckties
are widening and narrowing.

Lapels are widening
and narrowing. Collars
are buttoning up
and flying loose. Trouser
cuffs are folding
and unfolding. Skirts are
rising and falling, hair
is lengthening and shortening.

Somewhere, in the lamplight
of an apartment or hotel
room we once had, your
clothes are slipping down
again, my hands are going
crazy in your hair, our hearts
are beating against each other.

Somewhere surf is hissing.

Somewhere, Dover Beach
maybe, something fragile
and afraid is trying to last
forever.

Vicious Circling

I stand before
the neon wink
of a bar window
and think:
"I'll go in
and have a Scotch
drink and be
somebody.
Fulfill my
destiny." But
drawing from
my pants an old
Hoover flag
left over
from my father's
failed youth,
I see I lack
the least smudge
of a penny to pay
salvation's
cover charge
(a fin) with. So
I begin circling
the block
drunkenly, in
a holding
pattern, circling
the unattainable
earth.

Just Normal

for Bob Woolf

Now I don't care about hum-drum
order any more than
you do. I sympathize
with Huck Finn's taste for
the mixed-up. This is no
tight ship. I wouldn't
want my moments run off on an
assembly line like toy ducks. That's
not the point: it's been
raining possums for a month. And now,
when I'm absolutely up to my neck in
a whole bathtub of concerns, you
walk in unannounced, wearing
an ETERNITY sweat-shirt and leading some
kind of out-of-date dog on a leash, and
shake my slippery hand and tell me
"Just normal, thanks." Well, no
thanks. I've had enough. I'm going to
pull myself up over the side, and get
all the way out of my mind.

2900 Prytania

For Harwood Koppel

These top few
lines sagging
with words
like *ennui*
lagniappe
creme de menthe
constitute
the wrought-iron
balcony
of a poem
shaped just like
my new 120-
year-old house
in New Orleans:
a wooden lime
peel hanging
out of a lightning-
murdered tree
2 stories
down to knock
against
a honeysuckle-
scented neighborhood
of weird readers.

Park Bench Poem

Mind if I put up
a park bench
in your mind?
I mean, if
the mind is a park,
why not have a poem in it?
After all, when
you get through
buying hotdogs &
getting a load
of the swans
you'll want
some place to
sit down. It
ought to be fairly
comfortable by
the time a few
generations of
transient assholes
have worn it
smooth, & the paint
off— though
the original idea
was to advertise
my product: my own
green life, now
flaking into winter.

At 32

My poems used to be
as tense as boxers
(remember?) but
they don't stay
in the ring long
nowadays. They've
gone languorous
on me. All they
want to do is
drink gin & read
biographies of
Gene Tunney. They
tend to curl up
like doodle-bugs
& go to sleep
on the top line.
You probably
ought to consider
this one, for
instance, not
the "trenchant
commentary on
modern life" you've
come to expect, but
a picture postcard
from sunny Catatonia.

Gatsby

for Celia

Stanley Jupp,
Limmie Shorts,
Ollie Weary,
Donald Sixkiller,
Frederick Hotstream,
Prosper Sick,
Lazarus Loxfinger,
O'Neil O. Bush,
Daix Gunn,
Sophie Corner,
Ophelia Slain,
A.B. Close,
Irma Signal,
Fences Quaid,
Orlando G. Bendana,
the Quackenboss boys
(James, C.A. and John),
Hart Pillow,
Violet Pinkney,
Dewey Doggett,
Fanny Shoulders
and the whole
New Orleans
telephone book
came to the poem
I threw, hoping
you'd drop by.
Where were you?

Anonymous

i sent my Shell card back
with a small check to show my good faith
then i sent my Bank Americard back
with the minimum monthly payment
then i cancelled my life insurance
sent the Dallas lawyer all i had
declared myself bankrupt
then i sent back my driver's license
social security card
birth certificate
then i sent my old wallet flopping
into the brown river
now when i lift my hand the sunlight
pours right through it
now there is no one left for you not to love

Thirteen Ways of Being Looked at by a Possum

1

I awake, three in the morning, sweating
from a dream of possums.
I put my head under the fuzzy swamp of cover.
At the foot of darkness two small eyes glitter.

2

Rain falls all day: I remain indoors.
For comfort I take down a favorite volume.
Inside, something slimy, like a tail, wraps around my finger.

3

Hear the bells clang at the fire station:
not hoses, but the damp noses of possums issue forth.

4

Passing the graveyard at night
I wish the dead would remain dead,
but there is something queer and shaggy about these mounds.

5

From the grey pouch of a cloud
the moon hangs by its tail.

6

At the cafeteria they tell me they are out of persimmons.
I am furious. Who is that grey delegation
munching yellow fruit at the long table?

7

I reach deep into my warm pocket
to scratch my balls; but I find, instead,
another pocket there; and inside, a small possum.

8

My friend's false teeth clatter in the darkness
on a glass shelf;
around them a ghostly possum forms.

9

At an art gallery the portraits seem to threaten me;
tails droop down out of the frames.

10

I screech to a stop at the red light.
Three o'clock, school's out:
eight or ten juvenile possums fill the crosswalk.

11

Midnight at Pasquale's. I lift my fork,
and the hard tails looped there
look curiously unlike spaghetti.

12

When I go to the closet to hang my shirt on the rack,
I have to persuade several possums to move over.

13

Drunk, crawling across a country road tonight,
I hear a shriek, look up, and am paralyzed
by fierce headlights and a grinning grill.
I am as good as gone!

Moondog

for Louie Skipper

After midnight,
trying to sleep
(that is to say
having passed out)
on the living
room sofa, I
am aroused by
dogs barking far
away, like bells.
How far? Up on
State Street? or up
on Carrollton
Avenue? or
even across
the Lake, in some
strange parish? Or
is it some poor
Russian mutt stuck
on the moon who
wants Out/Off/Home?
No, I know now—
It's you, Louie,
on your hands &
knees, out in one
of those square states,
baying your wish (&
mine) that you were
here.

New Orleans, 1976

Tick Tock

Go lie on a river bank
some summer afternoon
when little yellow leaves
are drifting down
hitting the green water
one after another,
tick, in no particular
order or hurry. Can
you believe in time there?

Or go inside a room
where there's a clock, shut
your eyes and listen:
that's just a nervous
tick, you'd never imagine
it was going anywhere.

Hold on, though. Listen
to one with a tock too,
a tick tock: that's
more than nerves,
that's concern. It may be
a man with a wooden leg
running after you,
shouting You left me
back there on
the river bank, you took
my medals, you got old.

Late at Night

After I tuck Thomas Hardy away
and yawn and call TV talk
banal all the ways I can think of,
and stick a pipe in my mouth
and finally shut up,
there is a lot of
extra-conscious traffic
outside: the wind bulges
against the door, cats yowl,
and later the shades in the bedroom
crook in like knees.
The radiators groan Oh God.
And while my baby and I lie
bumper to bumper, history
starts up again: this time
it's stovepipe hats
cluttering down the courtyard.

The Sense of Decorum in Poverty

I put on a shirt
with a couple of
gone buttons and a
pair of pants my wife
hates and walk into
the living room and
sit down in a dull
chair. In this way I
acknowledge nothing's
going on. If I
wanted to really
suffer I could go
lie down in some shit,
but that transgresses
the fine line between
propriety and
masochism. If
I were any kind
of poet I'd go
stick up a Jiffy
Mart or, say the First
Bank of the Cosmic
Imagination.
Then I could buy a
red plaid jacket with
a rooster tie and
stumble out into
the clear autumn air
crowing "Guilty! Life,
I'm your beautiful
man."

"Cruising Down the River

on a Sunday afternoon…"

                    When I heard
that song as a boy in Alabama
I always thought: How could they do that?
It had to be illegal. Because
up there, among the red clay hills
and pine trees, everything was.

And anyway, Sunday afternoon
was for visiting, in hot little wooden
houses with a lot of
rocking chairs that were going
nowhere fast but the pearly gates,
and didn't know
I was a rebel against
the confederacy of the saved: I wanted to be
wearing a monocle and drinking
neon COCKTAILS, leaning on a lamppost
on the broadest boulevard in hell,
or cruising down the river
to heaven between your legs.

Urban Maudlin

Is it the accumulated
effect of the screwdriver,
bourbon on the rocks,
Dixie beer and three brandies
I've had today that
has caused the first
g to be torn from the
Pi gly Wiggly sign across
the street from this bar?

I don't think so. The red-
brick building is empty,
anyway, the plate glass dark
except as it reflects
the traffic on St. Charles.

The Battle House in Mobile
is empty too; and just
last week I read where the
Southern Crescent is to be
discontinued, or taken over
by Amtrak. Groucho Marx

is dead. Elvis is dead.
My drink is almost gone.
How sad! how strange!
that life should be
a tearing down, a closing
out, a flop. And our

great love, that boomed
and bustled once— is it
like downtown Mobile now—

empty, up for lease,

and dangerous after dark?
Or is it like Tuscaloosa
on a Sunday— closed? One
last possibility: Nashville,
where there's no place to turn.

New Orleans
for Ralph Adamo

From the air it's all puddles:
a blue-green frog town
on lily pads. More canals
than Amsterdam. You don't
land— you sink. When
we met, you, the Native, shook
your head. Sweat dropped
on the bar. You said:
"You're sunk. You won't
write a line. You won't make
a nickel. You won't hit
a lick at a snake in this
antebellum sauna-bath. You
won't shit in the morning if
you don't wake up with
your pants down." And you
were right: Three years later
I'm in it up to my eyebrows,
stalled like a streetcar.
My life is under the bed
with the beer bottles.
I'll never write another line
for anything but love
in this city where steam
rises off the street after
a rain like bosoms heaving.

The Great Man's Death: An Anecdote

The famous poet Everette
Maddox had been advised
by a team of wrong-headed
specialists that one more
snort of the Devil's Brew
would turn his lights and
livers puce. Nonetheless,
he awoke one night in a
borrowed flat with
a surging boredom on—
his only love at a permanent
remove— and got up
and strode the 20 or 30
blocks to Tyler's Bar,
where he had "Four hundred
and seventy-two Margaritas,
straight up, on Bank
Americard. I think that's
the record," he said, and
dropped dead, into a biography.

The Job

It looks like rain
and that's not
the worst of it.
But in a dream
I get a job.

It happens like this:

Out of the shadows
that fall across
gay umbrellas
welcoming me to
the Republic
of Cinzano, a face
smiles at me
sweating in my one
good wool suit
(it's 75 degrees),
and says: "You
look good enough
to eat. Good
enough to live;
yes, good enough
to work here.

"Despite your
M.A. in Volapük
from a possum
college and
Last Book Read
('Remembrance of
Things Past'), I
can tell somehow,

perhaps from
the excrement in
your eyes, you
are definitely
not overqualified
to sweep the butts
out of our
luxuriant patio,
day after day,
at minimum wage,
forever. But be
of a single mind:
You must not yet
be thinking
of marriage."

At Tin Lizzies

Having my first
drink of a long
spring day at
5 o'clock on
the plank patio
of this college
bar, a gold leaf
sky going up
behind the fence
over the tops of
the houses and
trees, I find
I have a bad
case of what
Huck Finn calls
the fantods.
Here, everybody's
in Accounting:
They wear yellow
pants and have
fat butts. They
go Beep. If
this is English,
or any other
language, I don't
speak it. Rodney
Jones said East
St. Louis was
the farthest from
home he'd ever
felt, but he was
never here.
A breeze blows

the napkin off
my table and I
suddenly feel
I'm on the deck
of a boat in
a storm— alone,
scared, missing you
across town.

Front Street, New Orleans

Everything is coming and going
at once in the hot June
sunshine though it's hard to say
which is which   A black trainload
of AMOCO crosses left in front of
a steamboat getting ready
to move out to the right   A girl
in a blue slit dress has her
own angle toward and past me with
a starched white boyfriend   Trees
nod   A busy moment in which
I do not forget to love you or
spill my coffee   Only Governor
Bernardo de Galvez who played
"so decisive a role" in the War
for American Independence
just off the ferry from Spain
on his horse looks indecisively
over my head up Canal Street
as if to say Where can a man get
a drink in this part of History

Southern Eclogue

I sat in Woolworth's for three months
and watched Summerama
turn into bright green Dollar Days,
although, as Ira Gershwin
would say, not for me. Out on
the street it was Dog Days. Dog-tired,
dogshit out of luck, and a little
mad, my new love dying
on the vine, I was what they call
self-employed, kicking my head
ahead of me down the sidewalk
like an old magnolia blossom
through the dust. Around the corner
a trumpet was talking to itself.
And up, up, up the alley cracks,
over the pink roofs of shut
stores, the Dog Star gave one
yelp and sank to sleep
as the Man in the Full Moon,
coming on, yawned in the pearling sky.

Twilight on the Verandah: Poem for Banjo

Dance you blue firefly
glowworm
lightning bug
moth
moonbeam
Japanese lantern
will-o'-the-wisp
with somebody else
I'm only a shuffler myself
and if I touched you
you'd pop
like a lovely party favor
all over Oak Street

The Time Between

This is the time I spend
getting up the nerve
to ask for a third
pack of Woolworth's
sugar for my coffee,
dangling in the bathtub
like a jellyfish, or
hunting the mantels
for a safety pin
to close up the hole
in my pants pocket
with, finally settling
for a paper clip,
deciding I need my pants
pocket closed up more
than I need my papers
together, as I must go
out! out! out! down
four blocks of public
sunshine, past crazy
women and bums,
to sit in the bar
all afternoon,
gritting my teeth
against the drink
somebody may buy me.

Is this what the Depression
was like? Is this
what death is like?
Am I depressed
or dead? And do I win
a grilled cheese

if I guess? Thunder.
The clock says five
after one, but I know
what time this is:
intermission at a cheap
play with the Coke
machine broken. The time
between wars. The time
between whatever
I used to do— pay bills,
fumble with purple
memos in a fluorescent
office, love you—
and whatever comes next,
or nothing: Venice,
crumbling into a blank sea.

The Milamo Bird

for Kent Ashworth

Kent, when questioned
on your rumored
bagpipe expertise,
you had to say
Nothing to it, but
on second thought
you added that
at one time you
had milked a lot
of cows. Well,
there you have it:
leave it to the truth
to get out of hand,
especially in here.
But Kent, the rumor
being false, or an
embellishment, what
was that raucous
tune volleying
down the bar? Oh
not the cry
of the Milamo bird,
flying backwards
into the swamps
of your Florida boyhood
fifty years ago,
and whistling through
its asshole, but
the most famous laugh
on Oak Street.

Even Odd

for my poetry students at McMain-Spectrum
Junior High School, New Orleans, October
1980

There go the days
like a stick on a fence:
even odd, even odd,
into winter.
When were you born?
I was born in October.
Is your birthday a banner
in the summer sky?
Where do you fall?
Are you the odd one in line?
If you told a kid that
he'd laugh.
But that's the language
doing that. That's
the language
making you laugh.
Put a hand over
your shirt pocket.
Can you feel that?
That's your heart
doing that.
That's your heart
laughing at the language.
The language wants
to love you: let it.

My Talent

somewhat after Chagall

It's true: I can't sing,
dance, whistle, make
coffee, change a tire,
or even pour piss
from a boot with any
accuracy. But look here:
if I stack these words
up just right
it may be you'll float out
the window and hover
for one instant
in the clear air
of my love, right over
the stopped clock
of the Whitney Bank.

Tropical

Outside it is so cold you feel as if a newly-
minted devalued nickel has been pressed against
your bare thigh until Thomas Jefferson looks up
from the silver lawn of Monticello and tells
you to beat it, brandishing his walking stick.
But a moment later in this dark green bar the
white-jacketed Negro waiter emerging from the
kitchen appears to emerge from a stand of
palms. It's the warmth from the unemployment
check burning a hole in my pocket that has
afforded us this metamorphosis. Gin rickeys!
I cry. Here in this booth our passion has
been reborn.

Sonnet Based on the Last Chapter of Booth Tarkington's *Penrod*

Somewhere beneath the murderous rock 'n' roll
pounding our century to powder, dear,
beneath the pinball screeching, can you hear
the quiet pleasures and fears of what I call
my love for you? Think of it as a small
town in Indiana. Summer. The year
1914, a little earlier.
No *Lusitania* yet. The Kaiser droll,
rattling his mustache to the Sunday band
concert in the park. Oh boyish love!
Such pleasure in the thought of you! and so
much fear, because what chance does a boy have,
so old, so little hip, that your little hand
will write him Penrod's message: "Your my Bow"?

Martini

It just hit me
not only is it stiff
it's cold
a poison ice cube
melting on top
of a one million
BTU Noilly Prat
window unit
dripping down the side
to hit me in the eye
repeatedly
where I lie on the floor
dressed in an olive
green business suit
arms folded
committing my favorite
warm weather form of
suicide to the theme
Willow Weep for Me

A Winter's Sonnet

My Louisiana wildflower, my palmetto
honey, my tropical wild blossom, my
European pastry, up a stump, I
feel like Judge Crater without you. So
have there been any calls? Even gumbo
has been devalued. That's not mystery,
that's confusion. A flawless blue sky,
there's mystery for you, a Tintoretto
of a winter's day. But, my daisy, blast
winter! screw death! Undevaluable star,
absent, of my cold nights, it's nobody's past
but an alcoholic clarity for us:
oh bring us drinks from wherever you are
and help me find the Spring in all of this!

Cleaning the Cruiser

The model of the cruiser *New Orleans*
is smaller than life
but larger than me. The glass case
with table stands six feet
seven inches high (I'm 5'8"
sober) and about fifteen
feet long. How I clean it,
once a month, on a small aluminum
stepladder, is, first, to brasso
the dim brass frame all over
with a rag— a pain in the aft,
as well as futile. Next, as to
the glass: one squirt of windex
under a paper towel becomes
a sort of filthy halo, a swirl
of drunkard's breath, which I rub
and rub, until at some point suddenly
everything disappears except
what appears to be nothing
but the reality of the fake
ship itself, its gray guns and planes
as plain as rain beneath my raised
hand… Dangerous point!
at which I imagine that I may fall,
or crash, through that drab
clarity, and hit the deck,
bound for the Philippines. Mean draft
indeed! into World War II,
which I only remember in sepia…
On the other hand,
talk about your escapes!
When the present storm is on, isn't
the violent past the safest place to be?

Oh I would do it— run away
and fight my father's war
all over again, to wear
the black gold-buttoned coat
that hung in some dream-closet
of my childhood, and find, at armistice,
you. Kiss me once,
I'd say, and kiss me twice,
and kiss me once again,
it's been a long, long time.

Conversation With Myself at a Street Corner

I'm glad I caught myself
quivering here at the corner
trying to get across
the summer day to the branch
library. I wanted to ask me
a couple of questions, *viz.*:
Old Son, what interests
you about this or any
other moment of your or
anybody else's life? I mean,
I seem to detect a sort of
dull gleam running around
your general haggardness
like Scotchlite on a bike.
Well, ahem, since I ask,
I'd have to say
the impingement of Fate on
quotidian activity is
something I have always
kept abreast of, and I am
BEAT. And conversely,
the scampering of the quotidian
across the face of Fate
like squirrels in a yard.
I prefer that order.
My opinion of Heaven
is roughly Mark Twain's:
I won't even stay where *I'm*
singing. Why, fuck wings!
We got public transportation
down here! If I had my way,

my every thought would be
a stained-glass window
in a modest mansion, to which
I'd return each twilight
to my sweet baby— though
she's presently doubtless out
with some goddam brain surgeon.
But I'll have to excuse me:
the light is changing,
and I must be run over
by the shadow of a streetcar.

Quest

There must be some place around here
we can do it. Not
the mezzanine, as the cigar stand

is still open, and we don't intend
to amuse passers-by through
Tampa Nugget fumes. Holding

your hand, our footsteps
ringing on stone stairs where
busts hang in the dark like

dead jack o'lanterns, I feel
sought after, called upon,
desperately happy. The perfect

place is somewhere: the Palm Court,
sliding down the laundry chute
(moving targets), on a burgundy rug

looking up at the lobster tank.
Now two big aluminum doors
swing open, and we are in a room

full of steam, where fish are
being scaled: scales falling everywhere
in the bright steam, arpeggios,

a shower of gold. We forget
entirely about doing it, hungry
for each other. This must be the place.

Approaching the Solstice

Canal Street sizzles
like an egg on the grill:
high in the nineties.

Jesus! a man would have to be
crazy, or in his sixth
childhood, to fall in love again
in this town in the summer!

But nobody ever learns
anything— that's what
tragedy teaches. So
my hottest wish now
rather figures: to get
out of the frying pan
and into the fire
under your cool white dress.

The September Sonnet

The maples are turning all the way down to the River,
the only thing that turns in this sluggard city,
but my heart is singing some old Gershwin, pretty
suspicious behavior. Do you suspect? Do the silver
skyscrapers know? Oh what could this Fall ever
have meant but my love for you! Why is the steady
urge of the ferryboat toward me making me giddy
except that I want to go on a boatride over
the glitters into the dangerous evening with you,
you, you, princess of the business district, sweet scrap
of the harvest moon we missed together, soft pulse
jumping like traffic through my day to a few
drinks. Exciting public love! may I still hope
we may share a shadow before there's nothing else?

The Wartime Sonnet

It was September in the rain the day
I had to leave you in the bar and go
to the editorial wastes. It was Hello
and Goodbye for us. Then I was out on the gray
pavement in somebody's car sliding away
from your face in the window. It was all so
dramatic! Oh the *Warsaw Concerto* was
playing and bombs were breaking and they
were stacking up the streetcars while twilight
spread like a lovely rumor over the shiny
city! That was in wartime! Or perhaps
all of those things are only things that might
have happened: all I remember is the tiny
drop of my Scotch dividing on your lips.

The Saddest Song in the World

In my opinion, the saddest song in the world
is Victor Herbert's "Gypsy Love Song."

We used to sing it in grammar school
to Mr. Donald Carr's piano.

Mr. Carr had oily black hair,
a black moustache, a red '56 Thunderbird,
and drank at the Highway Café
on Friday nights.
He was the most exciting man in town.

When we sang "Gypsy Love Song"
it was always winter.
His violin class played it too.

Emily Dickinson was right
about that "certain slant of light,"
but, Jesus, she should've heard
"Gypsy Love Song" just once,
creaking along a violin.
That's despair for you.

My whole life, the whole
effort of my life, has been directed
against that song— that bramble,
kudzu choking my heart,
and my friends' hearts.

Have I weakened? have I given in?
I wonder, driving home today
through the fall twilight,
up Freret Street, past

Frank's Steak House, past La Triana's bar,
past the Speed-Wash, the plant shop
with the fried chicken sign, singing

softly, for the first time in years,
"Slumber on, my little gypsy sweetheart,
wild little woodland dove..."

Armistice Day

In the 11th hour of the 11th day of the 11th month
Kaiser Bill threw in the towel,
threw in his spiked helmet,
said, "I'm gone to Holland,"
said, "Ain't gone study war no more."

Bill, I can dig the fact
that without some kind of serious reinforcement
the mortal scuffle is too much.

I'm standing in front of the liquor store now,
which is closed because it's Armistice Day,
which has been changed to Veteran's Day,
which has been moved to October 25th,
because your trip struck someone in power
as archaic.

Bill, I don't care: I know
how you felt when you fled across the Rhine,
soggy, without benefit of reindeer.
I'm through, too:
ain't gone study war, nor love,
nor anything now, except snow and the other
obvious trappings of despair.

Sonnet For Muzak

Something stops. But what? Not the carpeted
elevator. My heart. And starts again,
plunging, a roller coaster. Not in pain,
where I want to be, but in terror, a lead
balloon. Why? Because suddenly a sad
fiddle has crawled out of the walls. That's when
my lately sunlight-dazzled hair and skin
begin to prickle as if an empty bed
were going up under my coat. It's true!
they're playing "You'll Never Know" on the muzak!
They said it! those computers, wordlessly
confirming what I knew, darling, that you
won't, not ever, impeccable melody,
falling like rain beyond my poor lyric.

The Poem

It's a rug: jump
on a bump and
another humps

up. It won't stay
smooth. It's nice skin
that keeps breaking

out in boils. It's
a cathedral,
with every word

a little gar-
goyle. A big grin
with all the teeth

snaggled. Because
somewhere, down deep
inside, every-

thing is not all
right.

Breakfast

Oh hush up
about the
Future: one

morning it
will appear,
right there on

your breakfast
plate, and you'll
yell "Take it

back," pounding
the table.
But there won't

be any
waiters.

Hearing It All

For years you've heard life
talking low in the background,
but you've never quite understood
what it was saying. Then one day
you think maybe you just haven't
been listening closely enough,
or maybe you haven't really
been paying much attention
at all. So you stop and listen
closely, and strain to hear. And suddenly
you hear it all, and you understand
EVERY WORD OF IT, for the first time.
And the last. Because
while you're standing there
in the middle of the street, listening,
a big bus with a beautiful
green CUTTY SARK sign down the side
lumbers over you, and leaves you
mostly pavement.

Bean-Out

For the night's affair
I put on dignity
from head to toe. But
as I gesture before
the mirror's gleaming
teeth with a spoon,
I spill the beans
all over. Oh not
all the perfumes
of the five-and-dime
avail! And later, it is
as I feared. The
foyer's lights are
hard. The waiter's
disapproving eye
dribbles down my shirt-
front, and his compass finger
says Out. He has
a point: the stained
self will out, and must find
it's own way in the dark.

Crunch

It's me: I'm down here
near the bottom
of the barrel of light
the July afternoon's
dumped in my kitchen,
eating a sandwich,
hamming it up
for my gross buddy
the Body. That's right:
the crunch is me,
moving through toast
like an old radio
dial through static,
laying the lettuce
in the aisle. I'm
not the only one,
either: the neighborhood's
a sagging network
of stomachs; every green
shutter'd duplex is
a plant for the processing
of sentiment into shit
into— What? What's
this? High above the dogs,
chimneys, mimosa fuzz, up
in the blue air,
a man named Mahler
floats, drunk with song.

In the Dark

All of a sudden,
four o'clock
one afternoon, the lights
go out. Now I'm not
afraid of the
dark, but I'm working
on my stamp
collection, and I've
dropped it all
over the floor. Where's
the fuse-box?
I blunder across
the room, falling
flat on my face over
what feels
like a giant eel.
No fuse-box, I can't
find it. I crash
through a hatrackload
of snow-apples
and other bric-a-brac,
to the window,
my eyelid, and heave
it up. Now I'm looking
out of my head, and
it's simply pouring down
little snapshots
of you.

God's Last Words to the Stars

Coming home from beer with a beer
I hear the brain cells popping off
one by one like firecrackers

The stars going out one by one
leaving the sky black

God sweeping the last stars
under the celestial rug

Muttering not Good riddance
to bright rubbish but (more kindly)
Out of sight out of mind

Royal Street, Corner Conti

Hot day with clouds.
One of them brooding
days. One of them
magnolias sagging
onto the roof of one
of them sidewalk bars.
One of them old grey
folk singers out there
on the street. A lot
of them tourists,
with an admixture
of them lovers. One
of them invisible
pigeons just pissed,
straight down, narrowly
missing putting out
my pipe… Oh it's one
of them days that
threaten not to explode
but to implode, or out
of which the bottom
proposes to drop.

Dates

Ah yes, I remember them
well— my only talent.
Most of them are easy,
like Feb. 22, Washington's
Birthday (Old Style),
which is also my mother's,
and my parents' wedding
anniversary. Or July 14,
when my wife's and my
own brief reign of terror
and beauty began. I
know where I was on every
July 4 for the past eight
years— last year was
the best. Oh I may
hesitate a little over
moveable feasts, like
stepping on an escalator,
but by and large I know
these blazed trees when
I see them. But after
I brag to a bartender
that it was today, April 12,
in 1861, that the Great
Creole, Beauregard, put
the first pock-mark in
Ft. Sumter, he one-ups me
by pointing out tomorrow's
Friday 13. I don't
keep up with the future
so good. Good Friday

and a full moon, too.
And getting on the bus
tonight I am handed
a transfer to this effect:

APR 4 NAPOLEON
              12

Good Christ— on top of
everything else, I seem
to be invited to
the royal marriage of
April IV to Napoleon XII,
and me with my suit pants
in hock.

The Mississippi Sonnet

I don't care what they say about our River, Darling,
the wise guys: that it's full of spills and swills,
and everybody knows about the mud, that tells
us nothing. Look at it this Autumn morning:
silver in the sun, a handful of doubloons slung, gleaming.
It looks like the floor of Heaven. It fills
me with yearning. If I had the requisite skills
we could dance on the son-of a-bitch, careening
around like Fred and Ginger. But when I remember
I can't dance, oh my heart sinks and a bell
rings in Lloyd's of London and all Hell
suddenly breaks loose in the streets of November
because the thought of you and the attendant rage
at your loss is passing like a golden carriage.

A Double-Barreled Dud

for Paul & Dave

Brightness falls from the air
Thomas Nashe said.
That's you, Paul;
but when you brawl, Paul,
bring 'em red beans.
And when you rave, Dave
pat 'at bald spot
because it's always your shift somewhere.
And when all 'at friendship starts
give me a howl
& I won't fail to miss it.

What I Do

Somebody makes a crack like
"I'd rather have a bottle in front of me
than a frontal lobotomy,"
and I sieze that fleeting crack
and bang and hammer it, in a fury
of incompetent affection, until
it's fixed: an imperishable plank
in the platform of good feeling.
Oh, there's nothing to it, but
I do it well. So now
that I know what it is I do,
what my calling is, I hang out
my shingle. It reads: CRACKS FIXED,
and in more modest scrawl: Lines
End-Stopped While You Wait.

The Waste

As I sit here watching
the hands stagger around the clock
like one drunk following
another home, I ask myself
what else I might be doing
with this day. But I don't know.

Later, as I clatter uptown,
my fist tightens
in the trolley strap. Why?
Because April's not this
avenue, a white-green
blur; nor October
a stained-glass blaze.

Not any more. No,
but every blesséd month
a wad of desk calender
leaves I've got to burn,
one by one, as fast as
I can, to reach Payday.

The New Odor

for Ralph

Alice spilled a big
bottle of Tobasco
sauce all over the floor
of the Maple Leaf Bar,
and mopped it up,
but not to the extent
that an exotic new odor
didn't continue
to permeate the place
when you walked in,
about midnight. It was
Evening in New Iberia,
and you loved it. Even
the lepers danced (though
only with one another).
You left in a pirogue,
picking your teeth
with a fiddle-bow ("Hot
damn!"). And I, on
hearing your report,
thought: How easy it is
to change the world!
All it needs is to
hit the sauce! Why
do I not now, without
delay, drop fresh ripe
red peppers, distilled
vinegar and salt on
my bland life? But
of course it can't be
planned. Old friend,
why can't we at least
make the right mistakes?

Disaster Poem

One February afternoon
it was Spring.
The air was as soft
as the glazing
on a doughnut.
In front of the bank
across from Palmer
Park where
the streetcar line
ends, an old man,
himself perhaps
softening in response
to the day, stooped
to get a 25¢ worthless
hippy newspaper out of
a machine. He
dropped his cigar,
lighted, in, &
in the contagious
manner of
combustibles, paper
after worthless
hippy paper took fire,
& the old man's
400% polyester suit
followed, as did
the old man. Off
by the Lake
they looked up & saw
the lyric sky
smeared red like
a candy apple & said
"Another dumb

anecdote's turning
into a poem down at
S. Carrollton & Claiborne."

The Old Man Croaks

The old man croaks
"Noospeppa"
from his blue *Times-Picayune* stand
& matching blue & white umbrella
as clump after clump of real people
drift into the bank
in their tassel shoes
& I sit here on the stoop
all raggedy
wondering whether
with my lousy eyes
I can clean my fingernails
sufficiently
to buy a drink
from your pretty hands
when the corner bar opens.

How I Start My Day

First I go through the line
at K&B
& get a pack of matches
Next I go to Woolworth's
& drink 3 cups of coffee
& look longingly
at the little bottles
of pineapple juice
on the shelf
That takes care of that pack of matches
so then I go
back to K&B
& go through the other line
& get some more
This is all planned out
see
& that's just how it starts
& they say I ain't organized
They said that about Whitman too
but man
you ought to see his shoes
up there in Camden
Must be at least 20's

A Vision

I was sitting on the curb
by Dante & Oak
& in my mind's eye
or vice-versa
the hitherto locked
& jewel-encrusted
iron gates of your vagina
swung open
It was King Solomon's
   mines
& I was clinging like a bat
for dear life
to that golden wall

Courtin'

It was Sunday in the swamp
I was all dressed up
like Albert the Alligator
(handsome man look good
in anything he put on)
I said to the turtle
I said "Hand me that banjo
I'm goin' over to Suzy's house
and serenade her"
Turtle said "You goddam fool
you never played no banjo in your life"
& I said "Yeah
but you ain't seen Suzy
I'm gone play her
the complete works of Rimsky-Korsakov"

Happy Hour

Caroline
you little pressure
 cooker
I saw you bottle
 rocket
through the ceiling
 of the bar
like 151 exploded in a
 bar scotch bottle
your name & eminent
 credentials
appeared on the night sky
like the twice-per-century
 special
on the celestial black-
board

The Plumb Bob

Brent said "What's this"
holding it up
& I said "Beats me"
Brent said "It's a plumb
  bob"
& I said "All right"
& I thought of you sweet-
  heart
Wherever you are
& my heart falling straight
  & true
through your tits & ass
down to the parking lot
playing "Stardust"
as hard as it would play

Sunrise in Montgomery

Sucks
my heart up
through the vest
of my hand-me-up
little brother's 3-piece suit
I wore to the poultry reading—
Walt rolls goggle-eyed
with the post-excitements
Bill & Momo get it on
Ella on the tape sings
"The very thought of you"
Barb says "I wish I was on Baronne
    Street"
But I think she says
"I wish I owned Baronne Street"
& I think "Me too Hon'
we'd all be at the Fairmont
chawing diamond corn flakes"

Ordinary American Paranoia Revisited

After an hour on the bench
on the patio
in a paroxysm of love & lust
for you
I got up & staggered
down Oak Street
to buy some matches
for the bar
& it wasn't that I forgot about you
for an Einsteinian micro-second
It was just that they
were tearing up the streets
& I was so temporarily distracted
by the undesirability
of having my own blood
spread over me
like salad dressing
by an 18-wheeler
that I became an ordinary
American paranoid again
for the time it took me
to get back
& fall in love with you some more

Why He Did It

My friend said "Worked offshore
what a bitch
five week stretch
like a dog
broke my back
swallowed bilge
kissed ass
hated God
puked five times a day
But when I climbed off the boat
to pick up that plump green check
I knew why I did it"

I thought "You simple fuck
you lucky fuck
to have a mangy broke
worthless old bastard friend like me
who wouldn't stoop
to pick up that butt
off the floor
unless he jolly well wanted to"

Oh Moon

Caroline said "Is this
  the geriatric ward
or what?"
& I said "I don't know
but I wish they'd
  change my sheets
& I could use a peach
  schnapps
Or anything in that vein"
Oh moon of Alabama

Gusts from Girls

There was gust in the
  air
On the way to the men's
  room
They was gusts from girls
There was one then there
  was another
They smelled so sweet
I could hardly piss
for thinking about them
Somebody said "That ain't
real
That ain't the way they
  really smell"

& I said "Real
Do you think *Life on the
  Mississippi* is real
Do you think the Gutenberg
  Bible grew on a tree
Do you think God wrote the
  Concerto In F single-
  handed
Don't kid me
Fella name of Gershwin
  had a hand in it
Besides
I like bus fumes too"

Houston

Oh when I burst on Houston
I thought looka dese topless towers
looka dese
aquatinted skyscrapers
Oh I done died & gone to Texas
Why can't we just stop right here
& get one 'em Exxon martinis
"Eh-oo Neh-oo," they said,
"Neh-oobody stops here,
everybody lives up in the Heights
where it's fourteen
sidewalkless blocks
to the nearest menthol stogie"

Rain from the Puffs

I'm hunkered here
with a pipe & a glass of
   scotch
as rain falls from the puffs
of a late September sky
Tabby's Refrigeration
   Service pulls up
They been needing Tabby
cooler's broke or
   something
Some Yankees come out
talking shit
about where they're parked
Yankees always got cars
the regulars all say
We been needing this
but I just wink
I didn't need it
I wanted this silver
   disbursement
onto the sidewalk of my
   middle forties

Weigh Not, Want Not

I dropped myself
like a feather
on the penny scale
at K&B
& it said "Deposit less money
you ain't even here yet."

How I Got In
For Wade

Well
I was hanging
up to my belt buckle in grief
outside the Muddy Waters
I had my dirty hands all over a
  lamp post
It looked so flooded with
friends in there
that I didn't see how
I was going to gain access—
Then somebody said
"Know anybody?"
I thought & said
"I know Wade"
& they said
"Well Wade on in"
& so I lit my torch
& shook a leg
& waded on in
& had a hell of a time

For Robin at 40

40
Shit
Chickenfeed
Time I turned 30
I shook so bad
Time I made 40
I had shook my shoes off
But I didn't feel a thing
Point is
Robin
Whichever way
You look through the telescope
You're looking at heaven

Bad Band

Strumming the blood
off their ignorant fingers
beating that garbage can
to a silver pulp
I guess I'm supposed to feel sorry
for these poor bastards
doing something bad badly
as hard as they can do it
to nobody
but us four at the bar
I've seen poets like that
They thought the fewer people
the hotter shit they were
I thought they ought to've been home
petting the Pekinese
Hey I'm no better
except I try to keep my big mouth
clamped on a swizzle-stick

Out of Season

Going to the men's room
I think I hear "Winter
  Wonderland"
on MTV
Thank God it's not
But word thought & deed
  you know
Le Dommage C'est Done
& I done committed
depression in my heart
The only thing worse than
  Christmas at Christmas
is Christmas in Sepdamntember
Oh I feel sorry for Jesus
But Jesus
I'm all booked up
still mopping August off
  my pagan brow

Me & the Dog & the Bone of Love

Well— I woke up on the sidewalk
next to a dog—
inadvertently I assure you—
& the dog said
"What's the problem pal?"
& I said, "Unrequited love"
& the dog said "Pretty?"
& I said "Pretty as moonshine
through a broken bottle"
The dog said "Sounds serious—
where's she at?"
I said "Across the street"
The dog said "Long way"
& I said in my best graduate school idiom
"An unbridgeable gulf"
Dog said "Well— want a bone?"
& I said "I got a bone on"
The dog said "Naw man—I mean to gnaw on"
& I said "Well dog—
considering the encroachment
of a solid black sky
unrelieved by her smile
don't mind if I do"

Closing Time

Oh it was din din
　din
When I was trying
　to sleep
on the bench
in the bar
cans & bottles
　boxes
were banging &
　clunking
& ashtrays were
going however
ashtrays go
& the only quiet
　thing in the house
was my heart
which had given up
　on you

The Dream

I dreamed we passed
  the rocks
& fell in love
You came home from
  singing
in your red dress
I was passed out cold
on the linoleum floor
of our lovely kitchen
I was wo' slap out
from vacuuming
the marble stairs
my favorite job
It's so easy

You woke me up &
  said "It's all right"
I said "What"
& you said "Everything"
& I blinked & thought
  about history
& said "Are you sure"
& you said "I'm sure"
& I said "In that case
if this ain't a dream
I'll eat a truckload of
  oatmeal in the morning
& you know how I hate
  that shit"

Here's to Falling

Here's to falling on your face
on the dance floor
in a self-extorted mess
of beer & glass
Here's to the fallses
of Niagara & Nocalula
Here's to Fall River
Here's to the fall of
the Rumanian Empire
starring Andrei Codrescu
Here's to falling off your own tombstone
Here's to lying in the grass
where it's good to lie
or be lain
or get laid
so wet & cool
Here's to falling
not failing
Nobody loses in my poems
My friends are the Mike Tysons of friendship
& they can whip your ass
Boss

Republican Toast

I said "S.O.B."
& Anne said "What's that"
I said "Schnapps on Brown"
& Anne said "We don't have that
  in England"
Somebody said "Where's England?"
& Dusty said "North of Atlanta"
& I said "Well
Here's to the goddam
Motherfuckin' shit-eatin'
Ball-bitin'
Crawdad-cornholin'
Republicans"
& we all had hazelnut

Ol' Nat

Nat Persackly
I remember him
He was one of them boys
used to buzz around tin pan alley
He wore a shiny suit
& played the trash cans
but soft you know
so the stars & the cats winked
  back & forth
He was from Short Pans New Jersey
a long time ago
but you know
how it all comes back

Untitled: Marti

Marti
The night your
dress fell open
on the patio
you were the
Carnegie Hall
of sex
All I saw
was Liberace
singing "Howl
Be Seeing You
In All The Old
Familiar Places"
All the way to the
bank.

Encore: Here's to My Friends

Here's to falling *off*
  a log
Here's to falling *over*
  the dog
Here's to *falling asleep*
Here's to *falling out of bed*
Here's to falling
to *Hell* "in a hand cart"
Whatever that means—
Here's to falling *from the sky*
  in a fiery Fiat
Here's to falling
  "to your doom"
out of a shoddy funicular
Here's to falling *in* or *out* of love—
Here's to love—
Here's to falling off the *shelf,*
  the ledge, the roof, the porch, the "wagon"
Here's to falling off a bar stool
like Lionel Johnson
or Lionel Hampton—
or whoever it was
Looka here
It's Suzy's shoes
She done kicked off
in a moment of *unimpairment*
Here's to falling rain, stars, night, stocks
  grades, panties, arches, London Bridge—
Here's to falling off the dollar bill
  like Billy Cannon-
Here's to falling *out* of a cannon
  like the Falling Zucchinis

The 2nd Fall of the South

I left my Confederate cap
on the ledge
in a men's room
in a bar
in Alagoddambama
& the South
which had risen again
to a modest height
fell in the urinal
& I beat it back to New Orleans
in a boxcar full of banjos

Where I Had Been

Well I was gone
from where I go
down there in New Orleans
must have been four or eight
   hours
probably seemed like years
to them
(I'm pretty popular down there)
& when I finely reeled in
they said "Where you been
fishing for compliments"
& I said "Naw
I been on my hands & knees
gnawing at the sparkles
on the sidewalk
in front of the movie
in Tuscaloosa"

Historical Poem

First we whipped
  the Germans
That was V-E Day
Then we whipped
  the Japs
That was V-J Day
Then it was Sunday
  & Mike said
"I ain't drinking
  nothing today
but orange juice"
So that was O-J Day
See
he was whipped
from a week's
  drinking

Rhett's Farewell

To look at me you'd never think
I'd been to Atlanta
But whenever I have
a brandy & soda
I'm back in the Parasol Bar
of the Hyatt Regency
& when they say
"That'll be umpteen"
I say "Frankly my dear
me & Scarlett owned this town
before you Yankees burned it down."

No S—y Here

Oh (I mean o) when it was spring
up there in Alabama
the birds rang like tricycles
everything was new

Come fall
you could watch the
   rosy stubble
from the roof
till my Daddy said
Get off that roof
it's rotten

& then I moved to
New Orleans
& gagged on magnolias

The Outbound Dog

My friend Tony
threw some Mardi Gras beads
around a yaller dog's neck
as was yanked to a trendy grey
Volkswagen in front
of the Maple Leaf Bar—
& then receded
leaving me slumped against the opposite wall—
I was drunk
I can't speak for the dog
but I said "Dog
the air wears thin
hot wire that son of a bitch
& high tail it
for points elsewhere
I think
I can take care of myself"

What I Said to the Sky

I reeled out of a 6-martini
candlelit dinner
& stood in the usual gutter
clutching what was left
of the 20th century
& looked up into a sky
the color of a bruise
It looked like Mr Hyde
in Classics Illustrated
& I shook my fist
at the God that had vacated years ago
overdue on the moral rent
& said "I came up a romantic idealist
& life has made me a mean
cynical pessimistic piss-ant
fuck you & the clouds you rolled in on"
& some wise-ass passer-by said
"But what about Suzy"
& I said "Suzy
blew the last blast
on my toy trumpet
that's all"

Composed on the Back of a Dark Green Muddy Waters' Poster

When I woke up on the batture
& you were not only gone
but had never been there
& I heard the aluminum
silence of the river
I was scared—
it wasn't *metaphysical*
exactly
I just thought they were firing
cannons over the water
to make Huck's carcass rise

Sydney

For the Sullivans

Well I always wanted to go on stage
So I went up there & went to sleep
Nothing else was going on
It was dark in my sleep
I didn't know whether I was going to
  Heaven Hell or Birmingham
But I kind of felt like Huck Finn
I just wanted a change
By & by I opened my eyes
& it was a bracelet of lights
Hanging off a kidney-shaped coast
& I said "What in the foggy blue-eyed
  world is this?"
& the pilot said "Sydney man"
& I said "All right boss, lemme off"

Home in Their Biblical Beds

The very spiritual
bodies of women
flow away
in white dresses
in Poe & Rosetti
The most famous
flow-away being
Millet's "Ophelia"
in the basement
of the Tate Gallery
How come people
don't really flow away
but grind & groan & crackle
& waste into a naturalistic stick
like my mother did
at St. Jude's
in Montgomery
20 years ago

How We Beat the Creeks

Thirty-plus years ago
Gen. Andrew Jackson
was burning up the swamps
fighting the Creeks
at the Prattmont drive-in
I was about six
downtown
We had a creek
Autauga Creek
They fished off the dam
Around the corner was the barber shop
My Daddy used to leave me there
It cost a dollar
& he had the dollar
I didn't mind
It smelled good in there
& on the metal footrest
my feet didn't quite reach
it said "REG U.S. PAT OFF"

Heaven

For my Mother & Rupert Brooke

Once upon a time
about the time
the beautiful storybook
of the 19th century
was blowing shut
England's green & pleasant land
was still a kind of heaven
to little boys & girls
entombed in Alabama

Over there in the books
they had harebells, blue bells
bar bells
foxglove & eglantine
whatever all that means
musk melon crouched
beneath every couch
sheep gnawed the knot-grass
the room shone like a shilling
in Flanders fields the poppies blew
Everybody had a rendez-vous with death
and only Joyce Kilmer had ever
seen a tree

My mother loved Rupert Brooke
as a girl
she liked to rip up
his tombstone
and paste it in her scrapbook
next to Joan Crawford.
Rupert Brooke thought heaven
was for fish

Maybe he had something
besides blood poisoning
then all hell broke down
like a cheap car
Sons a bitches got hold a the
wheel
& ploughed the blue
bells under
and there was no
more England
except on BBC
and my Mother died of the
late 20th Century
where heaven was a hospital

Well
sleep well sweetheart
over there
on that hillside
in Alabama
by the railroad tracks
in that long dress—
you ain't missin' nothin'

Things I'd Like to Do Preferably Before I Die

A) Get Suzy
B) Get drunk
C) Write some
    poetry
D) That's all
E) Wait a minute
    Wait a minute
    Wait a minute
one more
summer storm
would be nice

Flowing on the Bench

As I was going to sleep
on the iron bench
in the back of the bar
I felt all right
I felt I was joining something
Not the Kiwanis Club
No
I felt like one river joining another
I felt like the Mississippi
flowing into the Ohio
Right where Jim & I
passed Cairo in the fog
Right where the book got good

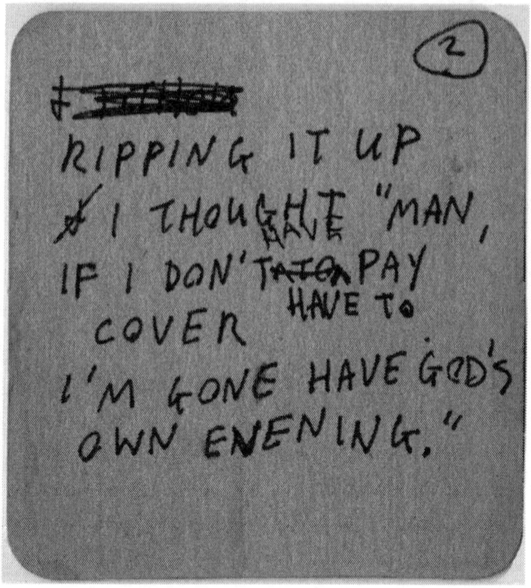
2
RIPPING IT UP
I THOUGHT "MAN,
IF I DON'T PAY
HAVE TO
COVER
I'M GONE HAVE GOD'S
OWN EVENING."

1
RIPPING IT UP
& I THOUGHT "MAN
IF I DON'T HAVE TO
PAY COVER
I'M GONE HAVE GOD'S
OWN EVENING."

Acknowledgments & Permissions

"Anonymous," "Armistice Day," "At Tin Lizzie's," "Balloon Piece," "Bean-out" "Breakfast," "'Cruising Down the River,'" "Crunch," "Disaster Poem," "Even Odd," "Front Street, New Orleans," "God's Last Words to the Stars," "Hearing It All," "Hypothetical Epitaph," "In the Dark," "Just Normal," "Lines on His Thirtieth Birthday," "Moon Fragment," "My Talent," "'No New Tabs,'" "Park Bench Poem," "Poem," "Publication," "Sonnet Based on the Last Chapter of Booth Tarkington's *Penrod*," "Southern Eclogue," "The Comfort of Artifice," "The Fighting Cereal," "The Great Man's Death: An Anecdote," "The Job," "The Miracle," "The New Odor," "The Poem," "The Substance of a Late-Night Phone Call," "The Time Between," "The Waste," "Thirteen Ways of Being Looked at by a Possum," "Tick Tock," "Tropical," "Twilight on the Veranda: Poem for Banjo," "Urban Maudlin," "Vicious Circling," and "What I Do" from *The Everette Maddox Song Book* (New Orleans: The New Orleans Poetry Journal Press, 1982) Copyright © 1982 The New Orleans Poetry Journal Press. Reprinted with permission of the publisher.

"2900 Prytania," "A Winter's Sonnet," "Approaching the Solstice," "Cleaning the Cruiser," "Conversation with Myself at a Street Corner," "Drinking Glass," "Heard (Glider) Poem," "Late at Night," "Maintenance," "Martini," "Monet," "Moondog," "New Orleans," "Of Fashion," "Of Rust," "Poem for Fred: On the Occasion of His Still Being Alive," "Quest," "Rutledge Youngblood Refuses to Lie Under the Banyan Tree Anymore," "Sonnet for Muzak," "The Blast," "The Milamo Bird," "The Reason Why," "The Saddest Song in the World," "The Sense of Decorum in Poverty," "The September Sonnet," "The Wartime Sonnet," "Welcome Home," and "What I Meant," from *Bar Scotch* (Paradis: Piroque Publishing, 1988) Copyright © 1988 by Everette Maddox. Reprinted with permission of the publisher.

of New Orleans Poetry, Mesechabe, The New Laurel Review, New Orleans Review, The New Yorker, No Comment, The North American Review, The Paris Review, Ploughshares, Poetry Now, Ponchartrain Beach: 50 Years of Fun, The Ponchartrain Review, Shenandoah, Solid Objects Cast as Goblins, Southern Poetry Review, Swallow's Tale, Tinderbox, Tulane Literary Magazine, Wavelength, White Mule.

E.H. Maddox
General Delivery
University, Alabama 35486
1

THE ANIMAL FAIR

By E.H.

Hatfield isn't much of
The capitals of Southern s
impressive-- except for the
of Atlanta, whose glitter'
that are still predominan
filthy. But Hatfield doe
that whatever infinitesi
ences there comes as a
The obvious way ir
is insufferably depres

The manuscript we are return-
ing to you is one in which we have
taken a special interest. Though
we cannot respond to each submis-
sion individually, we want you to
know that we are grateful for the
chance to consider your work, and
hope you will try us again.

THE EDITORS

with a young married woman. In fact, a woman married
to a highly respected citizen of Hatfield."

"Why--" I was unable to speak. The titles of
Wordsworth collections swam before my eyes.

"And furthermore, that you have been behaving in
a very disorderly and unacademic fashion. All this in
public. An extremely unfortunate situation-- for me,
as well as for you."

It really was the axe, then.

"But, sir, I-- who's been making these charges?"

He rolled his eyes up, then down, and tamped his
cigar ashes into a big tray.

"One of your own students, Mr. Barton. A young
man who has been in your class all year, and certainly
knows you when he sees you. Of course I cannot di-
vulge his name."

He didn't have to.

"You can see, Mr. Barton," he went on, "what a,
ah, predicament this puts me in. I can see no recourse
but to dismiss you from the faculty. I will speak to
no one further about the matter; there is no reason
for me to hinder your fortunes elsewhere. But I don't
see how we can let you remain at Holbrook."

"Dean Shank," I said, "I know who the boy is.
Surely you don't take this--" I wanted to say bastard.
"You don't take this sniveling whelp's word as ultimate

Alphabetical Index of Poems